SUPERSIZE
CROCHET

20 QUICK CROCHET PROJECTS
USING SUPER CHUNKY YARN

Sarah Shrimpton

sewandso

www.sewandso.co.uk

CONTENTS

INTRODUCTION

Welcome to the wonderful world of supersize crochet. Come in, kick your shoes off and have a look around. Things here are just like normal crochet but, erm, a bit bigger. That said, supersize crochet isn't all about making ginormous things (although there are a few large-scale projects in this book); it's about finding some truly chunky yarns and exploring different ways of working with them to create contemporary accessories for you and your home. In fact, it's about using everything you already know about crochet and pushing it to new limits. Like what you see? Well, the good news is that all you need to supersize your crochet are some chunky yarns and the biggest hooks you can get your hands on.

I should warn you, however, that it can be hard work; the yarn is sometimes tough on your fingers, the projects can be big and cumbersome to work with, and wielding a mammoth hook takes a little practice, too. (These most certainly aren't the sort of projects to take on your bus journey to the office.) But my goodness it's good fun; hard work it may be, but difficult it isn't. The projects in this book are simple, coming together very quickly, and enormous stitches mean that it's easy to see what you're doing.

So what can you do with supersize crochet? The answer is pretty much anything you like: make a cushion in a matter of minutes with some mega yarn; whip up a cosy blanket in a day; or create a statement beanbag with versatile T-shirt yarn. And don't forget that you can wear your supersize creations, too. Necklace? Hat? The cosiest cocoon shrug? They're all here, dear Reader. Supersizing your crochet doesn't mean that everything you make has to be massive, just that everything you make is awesome.

To supersize your crochet, the first thing you'll need are some mighty fibres. I've chosen a variety of different yarns for this book, all readily available (see my handy suppliers list at the end) and classed as 'super chunky' or 'super bulky'. Some yarns are acrylic-based (hard-wearing, vegan-friendly and cost-effective) and some have a generous smattering of wool content to keep you warm and add a touch of luxury. There's also plenty of cotton, including the on-trend T-shirt yarn (recycled and affordable) to provide structure for some of the larger projects. And there's one thing I can assure you: the only double knit yarn you'll find in this book is working extremely hard for the privilege*. And as for the hooks, most standard sizes up to 20mm (US size S/36) are readily available in your local yarn store. The bigger 25mm (US size U/50) and 40mm (no US size equivalent, just search for 40mm) ones are a little more special, but can be easily sourced online.

Supersize crochet is exactly what you'd expect; it's about creating show-stopping pieces which use chunky, mega chunky and truly mammoth yarns and changing the way you think about crochet forever. So what are you waiting for? Grab that yarn, arm yourself with that hook and let's make something superspecial.

*PS I have nothing against DK or any light-weight yarn. It's perfect for lots of wonderful crochet projects. It just doesn't cut the Supersize Crochet mustard without a little help.

Sarah xx

SUPERSIZE CROCHET TOOLKIT

The standard kit is what you'll need for supersizing your crochet, along with a few tweaks and some other essentials:

SCISSORS

A toolkit staple. Make sure one pair is heavy duty enough to cope with cutting tougher yarns and threads.

TAPESTRY / DARNING NEEDLE

The ends of giant yarns can be woven back into your work with your fingers, but you'll still need a sturdy tapestry or darning needle with a blunt end. Make sure you find one with a really big eye to make it easier when threading through those chunky yarns.

STITCH MARKER

To mark important stitches, often the first of a row or round. A large-sized one will be most useful, but you can always use a piece of coloured thread instead.

ROW COUNTER

Useful for counting your completed rows and rounds. Paper and pen work just fine, too.

TOY STUFFING / BEANBAG PELLETS

You'll need these to stuff cushions and pouffes. Each project will specify roughly what you'll need.

BUTTONS, RIBBONS AND OTHER PRETTIES

Most crafters I know have a rather large stash of these sorts of things. Useful for creating interesting detail on your finished item.

SAUCEPAN / LARGE MIXING BOWL

As crazy as it sounds, one of these is very useful for putting your yarn into to stop it rolling all over the place; standard yarn bowls are a tad small for most of the yarns in this book.

PLASTIC SHEETING / FABRIC SHEET

Some projects need a little protecting as you work with them. A plastic sheet (cut up a big plastic bag) does the job perfectly.

HOOKS

These are the most important pieces in your kit (alongside the yarn, of course). The projects in this book use big hooks. And some require mahooosive hooks. Each project lists the hook size needed and you're going to need:

mm	Imperial	US
4.5mm	7	7
7mm	2	–
9mm	00	M/N/13
10mm	000	N/P/15
12mm	0000	P/Q/16
15mm	–	Q/19
20mm	–	S/36
25mm	–	U/50
40mm	–	–

YARN AND ITS SUBSTITUTIONS

Each pattern specifies the brand and quantities of yarn you will need to complete the project, but what happens if it becomes discontinued, or if you want to try something different? To make it as easy as possible, a generic alternative is suggested – most projects, like the blankets, can be made with any yarn and hook size you like (even, dare I say it, double knit!) – simply follow the instructions in the pattern to adjust the number of stitches and rows to your liking. For other projects, try to source a yarn with a similar weight and meterage/yardage. That way, you'll get as close a match as possible.

HOME-MADE T-SHIRT YARN

If you happen to have a whole stash of unworn T-shirts (my kids insist on growing out of theirs) then you can make your own T-shirt yarn and it really is very easy (this works best with plain T-shirts, without a print on the front):

1. Lay your T-shirt flat and cut off the bottom seam and top section across the underarms. Discard these pieces (or, being the crafty person you are, repurpose into a fabulous accessory).

2. Make long cuts approximately 2.5cm (1in) wide from one side to the other, leaving a gap of about 2.5cm (1in) from the edge.

3. Open up the T-shirt and make diagonal cuts as shown to create a continuous length of fabric.

4. Wind this into a ball, stretching it slightly as you do so. The sides of the fabric will curl up and create T-shirt yarn.

Repeat for all T-shirts you find lying around the house – or threaten to. It's a good way of getting the family to tidy up, I find...

1.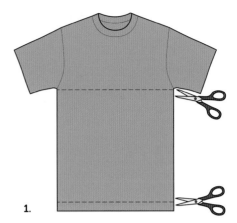

2.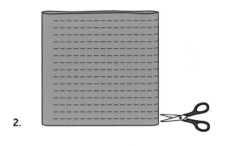

3.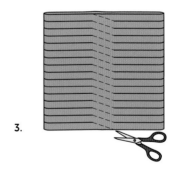

4.

TIPS FOR SUPERSIZE CROCHET

As a crocheter, you will already know how to hold your hook and yarn. And in essence, using a really big hook and yarn isn't much different. You'll just have to change things a teeny bit.

HOLDING YOUR HOOK

Big hooks take a bit of getting used to, but you might find the knife hold to be the easiest, especially for anything over 20mm (US size S/36). It will give you a bit more strength when you are pushing the hook into big stitches.

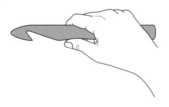

YARN FEEDING

This completely depends on what the yarn is like, of course. Chunky yarns can often be fed through your hand in the same way as usual, but you may want to work more slowly and loosely when using something coarse or bulky.

WORKING WITH TWO STRANDS

Some of the projects require crocheting with two strands held together. This is really easy. Simply find the end of two balls of yarn and hold them together; now crochet as normal. You won't notice much difference and the resulting chunky yarn is glorious. And what if you've only got one ball of yarn? Then find the centre-pull end and the outside end and use these together. The yarn rolls around a bit, so see the next tip, below.

WHERE TO PUT THE YARN

Some of these yarns are going to be pretty big. A trick which works for me is to wind the yarn into a ball and put it into a big saucepan at my feet. The pan helps the ball to roll as I pull the yarn, but also stops it from disappearing under the sofa. Bobbins of T-shirt yarn are also pretty big beasts, so you might want to stand them on the floor when you're working, too. The really ginormous yarns come in huge balls, which are very heavy. The best way to work with one of these is to put it in a bag on the floor and gently ease out a long length of yarn to work with – if you pull too hard, the yarn is likely to break, which is best avoided.

GO TO BED

No joke. Some of the large-scale projects are perfect to make in bed, where you'll have the benefit of much more space to support your work (remember I said that some get a little heavy), rather than letting it trail all over the floor. And it's a good excuse to find some peace and quiet, too.

WEAVING IN ENDS OF GIANT YARN

Let's face it, these mega yarns aren't going to fit through the eye of a regular needle, so just use your fingers to do the job instead.

PROJECTS

HANGING POUCH

Versatile and practical, this hanging storage basket is the perfect antidote to a cluttered bathroom, an untidy bedroom or a jumbled craft room. Use the loop and hang it on a peg or cupboard handle and stash away all those homeless nick-nacks. This pattern is worked in joined rounds of chunky cotton cord to create a rounded shape.

TOP TIP

I sometimes find that the ch-3 stitch at the beginning of each round can be a bit too tall. If you have the same problem, then simply chain two stitches instead. When you've finished each round, make your slip stitch into the top of the ch-2 to join the round.

OTHER THINGS TO TRY

You can make the hanging loop as long or short as needed: adjust the length of the chain in Round 13 and in the next round, make the same number of double crochet stitches in the ch-space.

YOU WILL NEED:

- Crochet hook: 7mm (US K/10.5 or L/11)
- 3 x 100g (3½oz) balls Katia Cotton Cord in Orange (shade 56)
- Tapestry needle

Yarn alternative:

Any yarn and hook to match

Finished size:

30 x 26cm (12 x 10¼in)

PATTERN

With 7mm hook, ch 4, join with sl st to make a ring.

Round 1: ch 3 (counts as tr here and throughout), 11tr in ring. Sl st into top of beginning ch-3 to join round. (12 sts)

Round 2: ch 3, tr 1 in same st at base of ch-3, 2tr in each st around. Sl st into top of beginning ch-3 to join. (24 sts)

Round 3: ch 3, 2tr in next st, *tr 1, 2tr in next st* repeat from * to * around. Sl st into top of beginning ch-3 to join. (36 sts)

Round 4: ch 3, tr 1, 2tr in next st, *tr 2, 2tr in next st* repeat from * to * around. Sl st into top of beginning ch-3 to join. (48 sts)

Round 5: ch 3, tr 2, 2tr in next st, *tr 3, 2tr in next st* repeat from * to * around. Sl st into top of beginning ch-3 to join. (60 sts)

Round 6: ch 3, tr 3, 2tr in next st, *tr 4, 2tr in next st* repeat from * to * around. Sl st into top of beginning ch-3 to join. (72 sts)

Rounds 7–12: ch 3, tr 1 in each st around. Sl st into top of beginning ch-3 to join.

Round 13: ch 3, tr 11, (tr2tog) 24 times, tr 12, ch 20. Sl st into base of ch-20 (this makes the hanging loop). (48 sts excluding the hanging loop)

Round 14: dc 48 BLO, dc 20 in ch-20sp. Sl st to next st to join.

Fasten off, weave in ends.

MAHOOOOSIVE BLANKET

I couldn't write an extreme crochet book without the word 'mahoooosive' figuring in it at least once. And here it's rightly deserved; this blanket is huge in scale (the entire family can fit under it), it uses enormous yarn and a great big hook. I'll let you into a secret, though – it's a ridiculously easy pattern and you can make this blanket in a day.

TOP TIP

This yarn is so thick that it's easier to use your fingers to weave in the ends, rather than wrestling with trying to thread a needle.

OTHER THINGS TO TRY

You can vary the size of this blanket easily. Just ensure that your foundation chain is an even number, and the pattern will work. Add or reduce the number of rows to make your preferred length.

YOU WILL NEED:

- Crochet hook: 25mm (US U/50)
- 12 x 300g (10½oz) balls Bernat Mega Bulky in Toasty Grey (shade 88017)

Yarn alternative:

Any yarn and hook to match

Finished size:

Approximately 120 x 190cm (4ft x 6ft 3in)

PATTERN

The (ch 1) at the beginning of Rows 1 and 54 is your turning chain and is not counted as a stitch.

Foundation ch: ch 38.

Row 1: (ch 1), dc 38, turn. (38 sts)

Row 2: ch 3 (counts as tr), dc 1 in 5th ch from hook, *tr 1 in next st, dc 1 in next st* repeat from * to * to end, turn.

Rows 3–53: (or until yarn runs out, leaving enough for final row) Repeat Row 2, working last dc into top of beginning ch-3.

Row 54: (ch 1), dc 38.

Fasten off, weave in ends.

STORE-ALL STORAGE BASKETS

I can think of a million uses for these. I'm sure you can, too, so I won't list them here. Let's just agree that most rooms would benefit from one. Or two. Or three. (Actually, definitely three.)

TOP TIP

The biggest basket is a whopper, so don't expect it to stand up on its own. Instead, fill it with all the stuff that needs to be stored and marvel at its capacity to hide away everything you don't want to see.

OTHER THINGS TO TRY

You can make the baskets whatever size you like by varying the size of the circles at the beginning of the pattern. Make a circle with the base size you want (ensuring the last round has an odd number of stitches) and then follow the pattern for the sides, adjusting the number of rounds to create the height you want.

YOU WILL NEED:

- Crochet hook: 9mm (US M/N/13)
- Large basket: 10 x 100g (3½oz) balls DMC Natura XL in Ecarlate (shade 05)
- Medium basket: 7 x 100g (3½oz) balls DMC Natura XL in Blanc (shade 01)
- Small basket: 6 x 100g (3½oz) balls DMC Natura XL in Lagon (shade 07)
- Tapestry needle

Yarn alternative:

Any yarn and hook to match

Finished size:

Large: 33 x 45cm (13 x 17¾in)

Medium: 29 x 43cm (11½ x 17in)

Small: 26 x 38cm (10¼ x 15in)

PATTERN

Hold 2 strands together throughout pattern.

Work in a continuous spiral.

LARGE BASKET

BASE

Round 1: In Ecarlate, ch 3 (ch 2 counts as a htr), 7htr in 3rd ch from hook. (8 sts)

Round 2: 2htr in each st around. (16 sts)

Round 3: *htr 1, 2htr in next st* repeat from * to * around. (24 sts)

Round 4: *htr 2, 2htr in next st* repeat from * to * around. (32 sts)

Round 5: *htr 3, 2htr in next st* repeat from * to * around. (40 sts)

Round 6: *htr 4, 2htr in next st* repeat from * to * around. (48 sts)

Round 7: *htr 5, 2htr in next st* repeat from * to * around. (56 sts)

Round 8: *htr 6, 2htr in next st* repeat from * to * around. (64 sts)

Round 9: *htr 7, 2htr in next st* repeat from * to * around. (72 sts)

Round 10: *htr 8, 2htr in next st* repeat from * to * 7 times, htr 9. (79 sts)

SIDES

Round 1: sl st to 3rd loop at back of next st. Turn over base so WS is facing. All stitches in this round will be made in the 3rd loop at the back of the stitches. Ch 2 (counts as htr), *sl st 1, htr 1* repeat from * to * around.

Round 2: sl st 1, *htr 1, sl st 1* repeat from * to * around.

Round 3: htr 1, *sl st 1, htr 1* repeat from * to * around.

Rounds 4–25: Repeat Rounds 2 and 3 alternately. (79 sts)

HANDLES

Round 1: sl st 1, ch 12, sk next 11 sts, (sl st 1, htr 1) 14 times, ch 12, sk next 11 sts, (htr 1, sl st 1) 13 times, htr 1, sk last st, sl st into 1st st.

Round 2: ch 2 (counts as htr), *16htr in ch-12sp, htr 1 in each st to next ch-12sp* repeat from * to * twice, sl st into top of beginning ch-2 to join.

Fasten off, weave in ends.

MEDIUM BASKET

BASE

Rounds 1–8: In Blanc, follow large basket pattern.

Round 9: (htr 7, 2htr in next st) 8 times, htr 8. (71 sts)

SIDES

Rounds 1–22: Follow large basket pattern.

HANDLES

Round 1: htr 1, ch 12, sk next 11 sts, (htr 1, sl st 1) 12 times, ch 12, sk next 11 sts, (sl st 1, htr 1) 11 times, sl st 1, sk last st, sl st to 1st st to join.

Round 2: ch 2 (counts as htr), *16htr in ch-12sp, htr 1 in each st to next ch-12sp* repeat from * to * around, sl st to top of beginning ch-2 to join.

SMALL BASKET

BASE

Rounds 1–7: In Lagon, follow large basket pattern.

Round 8: (6 htr, 2htr in next st) 7 times, htr 7. (63 sts)

SIDES

Rounds 1–20: Follow large basket pattern.

HANDLES

Round 1: htr 1, ch 12, sk next 11 sts, (htr 1, sl st 1) 10 times, ch 12, sk next 11 sts, (sl st 1, htr 1) 9 times, sl st 1, sk last st, sl st to 1st st to join.

Round 2: ch 2 (counts as htr), *16htr in ch-12sp, htr 1 in each st to next ch-12sp* repeat from * to * around, sl st into top of beginning ch-2 to join.

THE COSIEST SLIPPERS

I'm one of those people who wear slippers all year round; I simply cannot stand cold feet. And in the winter months, I don't just want warm toes, I want warm ankles too. Slipper boots are the only solution and perfect for keeping those icy chills at bay.

TOP TIP

This pattern is designed to fit a standard width adult foot and the slippers have a fair degree of stretch. To alter the length, simply adjust the number of rows as necessary – and continue with the rest of the pattern.

OTHER THINGS TO TRY

If you're worried about slipping over in your slippers, then apply dots of non-slip or slipper glue to the soles. Problem sorted.

These slippers can also be easily made without the boot cuff: make up to Round 1 of the Cuff pattern and you'll have a cute little pair of day slippers.

YOU WILL NEED:

- Crochet hook: 10mm (US N/P/15)
- 4 × 100g (3½oz) balls Drops Polaris in White (shade 01)
- Tapestry needle

Yarn alternative:

Choose a super chunky yarn which works to a similar tension with a 10mm hook

Tension:

Approximately 7 rows and 6 sts of double crochet to 10 × 10cm (4 × 4in)

Finished size:

To fit an adult size: UK 6 / US 8 / EU 39

Sole measures: 28cm (11in)

Floor to top of cuff: 19cm (7½in)

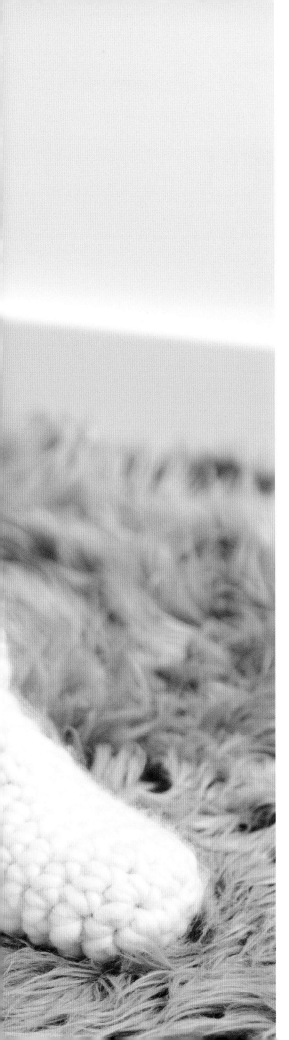

PATTERN (MAKE 2)

TOE

Work around both sides of the foundation chain, then in continuous rounds.

Ch 4.

Round 1: Beginning in 2nd ch from hook, dc 2, 3dc in next ch, turn to work along opposite side of ch, dc 1, 2dc in last st. (8 sts)

Round 2: *2dc in next st, dc 1* repeat from * to * around. (12 sts)

Round 3: *dc 5, 2dc in next st* repeat from * to * twice. (14 sts)

Rounds 4–8: dc 1 in each st around.

Round 9: dc 3, 2dc in next st, dc 1, 2dc in next st, dc 8. (16 sts)

Rounds 10–11: dc 1 in each st around.

FOOT

Work in rows

Row 12: (short row) dc 4 (leave 12 sts unworked), turn.

Row 13: (short row) ch 1 (not counted as a st here and throughout), dc 11 (leave 5 sts unworked), turn. (11 sts)

Rows 14–20*: ch 1, dc 1 in each st across, turn.

*or until desired length reached

Do not fasten off.

HEEL SEAM

Turn the edges with RS together and join the two sides with 5 sl sts. Fasten off.

CUFF

Round 1: With RS facing, and beginning in any stitch at the back of the foot, dc 1 in each st across the side edge, the front and the other side of the slipper. Sl st into 1st dc to join round.

Round 2: ch 3 (counts as tr), tr 1 in each st around (make sure you have an even number of stitches in this round – if not, simply work an extra tr in your last st). Sl st into top of beginning ch-3 to join.

Rounds 3–5: ch 2 (counts as a short tr), fptr 1, *tr 1, fptr 1* repeat from * to * around. Sl st into top of beginning ch-2 to join.

Fasten off, weave in ends.

MOROCCAN POUFFE

Inspired by the rich jewel-like colours of the markets and medina of Marrakesh, this pouffe combines a traditional way of crocheting with a new technique, resulting in another exciting project for your home. The top is crocheted separately, using extreme crochet's nemesis, double knit yarn*, in a surprising way.

*See, I told you that DK yarn has its uses and have graciously allowed it into my book – I've made it work hard for the privilege, though.

TOP TIP

Don't worry too much about the stitches I've prescribed for the top of the cushion. You may find that your T-shirt yarn is slightly different to mine and may need more, or fewer stitches per round. Simply adjust as you go.

OTHER THINGS TO TRY

Why not make a Moroccan-style rug to match the pouffe? Use the same technique as for the top of the pouffe and keep crocheting in circles until you have the right size.

YOU WILL NEED:

- Crochet hook: 4.5mm (US 7) for the top and 15mm (US Q/19) for the base
- 2 x 860g (30oz) approx bobbins of Tek Tek Yarn in Bright Pink
- 1 x 100g (3½oz) ball of Patons 100% Cotton DK in Teal (shade 2726)
- 1 x 100g (3½oz) ball of DMC Petra 3 in Gold (shade 53045)
- 350–500g (12–18oz) of beanbag pellets in beanbag liner, or cushion stuffing
- Tapestry needle

Yarn alternative:

Any T-shirt yarn plus any DK yarn

Finished size:

Approximately 44cm (17½in) wide by 20cm (8in) tall

PATTERN

TOP

Work in continuous rounds. From Round 2, you will make your stitches over the T-shirt yarn.

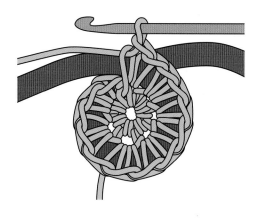

Round 1: In Teal, with 4.5mm hook, ch 2, 7dc in 2nd ch from hook. (7 sts)

Round 2: (over T-shirt yarn from now on) 2dc in each st around. (14 sts)

Round 3: *(dc 1, ch 1) in next st* repeat from * to * around. (28 sts)

Round 4: *(dc 1, ch 2) in next ch-1sp*, repeat from * to * around. (42 sts)

Round 5: *(dc 1, ch 1, dc 1, ch 1) in next ch-2sp*, repeat from * to * around. (56 sts)

Round 6: *(dc 1, ch 1) in next ch-1sp* repeat from * to * around.

Round 7: *(dc 1, ch 2) in next ch-1sp*, repeat from * to * around. (84 sts)

Round 8: *(dc 1, ch 1, dc 1, ch 1) in next ch-2sp*, repeat from * to * around. (112 sts)

Round 9: Change to Gold, *(dc 1, ch 1) in next ch-1sp* repeat from * to * around.

Round 10: *(dc 1, ch 1) in next ch-1sp* repeat from * to * around.

Round 11: *(dc 1, ch 2) in next ch-1sp* repeat from * to * around. (168 sts)

Round 12: *(dc 1, ch 2) in next ch-2sp* repeat from * to * around.

Round 13: *(dc 1, ch 1, dc 1, ch 1) in next ch-2sp, (dc 1, ch 1) in next ch-2sp* repeat from * to * around.

Rounds 14–15: *(dc 1, ch 1) in next ch-1sp* repeat from * to * around.

Rounds 16–17: Change to Teal, *(dc 1, ch 2) in next ch-1sp* repeat from * to * around. (252 sts)

Round 18: *(dc 1, ch 1, dc 1, ch 1) in next ch-2sp, (dc 1, ch 1) in next ch-2sp* repeat from * to * around.

Rounds 19–22: *(dc 1, ch 1) in next ch-1sp* repeat from * to * around.

Weave in ends on WS. Do not fasten off or cut yarn; you will crochet the top to the base later.

BASE

Round 1: In Bright Pink, with 15mm hook, ch 2, 6dc in 2nd ch from hook. (6 sts)

Rounds 2–3: 2dc in each st around. (24 sts)

Round 4: *dc 3, 2dc in next st* repeat from * to * around. (30 sts)

Round 5: *dc 4, 2dc in next st* repeat from * to * around. (36 sts)

Round 6: *dc 5, 2dc in next st* repeat from * to * around. (42 sts)

Round 7: *dc 6, 2dc in next st* repeat from * to * around. (48 sts)

Round 8: *dc 7, 2dc in next st* repeat from * to * around. (54 sts)

Round 9:** *dc 8, 2dc in next st* repeat from * to * around. (60 sts)

**continue to make increases until the base is the same diameter as the top.

Round 10: In BLO, 1 dc in each st around.

Rounds 11–22 (or until desired height is reached): 1 dc in each st around.

Fasten off, weave in ends.

TO MAKE UP

Have the base and top with RS facing out. You will use the Teal yarn and a 4.5mm hook to double crochet the stitches of the top to the inside loop of the top round of the base.

For each loop, make the following stitches: *4dc in each loop for the first four loops, 5dc in 5th loop* repeat from * to * around (adjust the number of stitches made in each loop if you have altered the pattern).

Once you're about half way around, insert the beanbag filling and continue to close the top.

Fasten off and weave in ends.

CONTEMPORARY WALL HANGING

Create a fabulously modern piece of artwork for your wall in no time at all using giant yarn, a big hook and an even bigger stick. Looking for that cosy, feel-good *hygge* vibe in your home? This might be just the piece for you.

TOP TIP

I sourced my stick from the local woods. You could do the same, or you could use a similar stick-type thing to hang your crochet from; if it's about 1m (1yd) long, you're good to go.

OTHER THINGS TO TRY

This giant yarn makes quite a statement and any motif would look stunning hung on the wall. How about a giant granny square? Or mix it up by combining all your favourite stitches to create a show-stopping piece of art.

YOU WILL NEED:

- Crochet hook: 40mm
- Stick (approx 1m/1yd) in length)
- 700g (24¾oz) Woolly Mahoosive Petite Merino Super Chunky Yarn in Cream
- 1m (1yd) of any DK cream yarn or string

Yarn alternative:

Any giant yarn and hook to match

Finished size (of crochet):

48 × 65cm (19 × 25¾in)

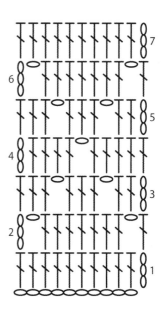

PATTERN

Ch 10.

Row 1: ch 3 (counts as tr here and throughout), 1 tr in each st to end, beginning in 4th ch from hook, turn. (11 sts)

Row 2: ch 4 (counts as 1 tr and 1 ch here and throughout), tr 7 (beginning in 7th st from hook), ch 1, sk 1 st, tr 1 in next st, turn.

Row 3: ch 3, tr 1 in ch-1sp, 1tr in next st, ch 1, sk 1 st, tr 3, ch 1, sk 1 st, tr 1, tr 1 in ch-1sp, tr 1 in 3rd of beginning ch-4, turn.

Row 4: ch 3, tr 2, tr 1 in ch-1sp, tr 1, ch 1, sk 1 st, tr 1, tr 1 in ch-1sp, tr 3 (working last tr in top of beginning ch-3), turn.

Row 5: ch 3, tr 2, ch 1, sk 1 st, tr 1, tr 1 in ch-1sp, tr 1, ch 1, sk 1 st, tr 3 (working last tr in top of beginning ch-3), turn.

Row 6: ch 4, tr 1 (beginning in 7th st from hook), tr 1 in ch-1sp, tr 3, tr 1 in ch-1sp, tr 1, ch 1, sk 1 st, 1tr into top of beginning ch-3, turn.

Row 7: ch 3, tr 1 in ch-1sp, tr 7, tr 1 in ch-1sp, 1tr into top of beginning ch-3.

Fasten off, weave in ends.

TO MAKE UP

Tie the end of the cream yarn or string to the stick and thread it through the top loops of the foundation chain and back over the stick until it is secured in place. Make a knot and trim the ends away.

Key	
⬯	Chain stitch
†	Treble stitch

JUTE PLANT HOLDER

You'll need to raid the garden shed for this project as it uses good old-fashioned twine – yep, it's the stuff Grandad uses to tie up his runner beans. I've taken my inspiration from those macramé plant holders from the 1970s, but brought it right up to date with a crochet hook. You'll work in continuous rounds, so use your stitch marker and you'll know where the first stitch of the round is. The hanging chains are added at the end and can be left off if you prefer.

TOP TIP

I cannot lie. Jute is a little tough on the hands. The best advice I can give is to work with fairly loose tension. And don't worry, this project doesn't take very long to complete.

OTHER THINGS TO TRY

Why not experiment with other twines and cords to make this plant holder? You'll need to experiment with hook size, but try it and see what works.

YOU WILL NEED:

- Crochet hook: 9mm (M/N/13)
- 1 × 400g (14oz) ball of 5-ply natural jute garden twine
- 9 × 2.5cm (1in) wooden beads
- Tapestry needle

Yarn alternative:

Any cotton yarn and hook to match

Finished size:

Plant holder: 16cm (6¼in) tall and 18cm (7in) wide across the top; hanging chains: 40cm (16in) long

PATTERN

Round 1: 6dc in magic ring or, ch 2, 6dc in 2nd chain from hook. (6 sts)

Rounds 2–3: 2dc in each stitch around. (24 sts)

Round 4: *dc 3, 2dc in next st* repeat from * to * around. (30 sts)

Round 5: *dc 4, 2dc in next st* repeat from * to * around. (36 sts)

Round 6: dc 36 in BLO.

Rounds 7–11: dc 36.

Round 12: *dc 5, 2dc in next st* repeat from * to * around. (42 sts)

Round 13: *dc2tog, ch 1* repeat from * to * around.

Round 14: *dc 1 in dc2tog, dc 1 in ch-1sp* repeat from * to * around.

Rounds 15–18: dc 42.

Round 19: ch 1, turn. Make reverse dc stitch around the top (see Crochet Stitches in Techniques).

Fasten off, weave in ends.

HANGING CHAINS (MAKE 3)

Cut 3m (3¼yd) of twine and thread three beads onto one end. Leave a 20cm (8in) tail at the other end, make a slipknot and begin crocheting. To add a bead, move it along the yarn up to the hook and create a big chain to fit around its circumference. Yarn over and pull the yarn through. Continue with the chains until you need to add another bead.

Ch 7, add a bead, ch 7, add a bead, ch7, add a bead, ch 7.

TO MAKE UP

Sew the three chains, evenly-spaced, just inside the top edge of the plant holder. Gather the ends and tie together.

PET BED

Make the cosiest of beds for your favourite furry pal using colossal yarn and a gargantuan 40mm hook. Crocheted in rounds to begin with and then rows, the pattern uses the centre double crochet stitch to give structure and strength to this eye-catching basket. Oh, and it takes about an hour to make... I kid you not.

TOP TIP

This yarn is truly mega and wonderful to work with. To prevent it from pilling as you crochet, put a sheet of plastic underneath. That way, as you turn your work, it will slide easily. You might also want to transfer this project to a table as it gets a bit big to handle on your lap.

If you find the stitches in the first rounds a little tricky to push that big ol' hook into, simply use your fingers to pull the yarn through the stitch and then insert your hook back into the loop to complete the stitch.

OTHER THINGS TO TRY

To adjust the size of the bed, leave out the shaping from Row 6 and either make it smaller, by stopping a round or two earlier, or larger, by continuing to make increases. Then carry on with the process in the pattern – decrease the circle to begin the sides, leave out some stitches to create the front opening, then crochet a few rows to create the height. Use my pattern directions as a guide and you'll be fine.

YOU WILL NEED:

- Crochet hook: 40mm
- 4kg (140oz) Woolly Mahoosive Mammoth Yarn in Turquoise

Yarn alternative:

Any giant yarn

Finished size:

55 × 50 × 20cm (21¾ × 19¾ × 8in)

PATTERN

Round 1: ch 2, 6dc in 2nd ch from hook. (6 sts)

Round 2: 2cdc in each st around. (12 sts)

Round 3: *cdc 1, 2cdc in next st* repeat from * to * around. (18 sts)

Round 4: *cdc 2, 2cdc in next st* repeat from * to * around. (24 sts)

Round 5: *cdc 3, 2cdc in next st* repeat from * to * around. (30 sts)

Round 6: *cdc 10, (2cdc in next st) 5 times* repeat from * to * twice. (40 sts)

Rounds 7–8: 1 cdc in each st around.

Round 9: (short row) cdc 2 (leave remaining 38 sts unworked), turn.

Round 10: ch 1 (not counted as a st), *cdc 2, cdc2tog* repeat from * to * around. Sl st to 1st cdc to join. Do not turn. (30 sts)

Row 11: (short row) ch 1 (not counted as a st), cdc 24 (leave remaining 6 sts unworked). (24 sts)

Fasten off.

Row 12: With RS facing, rejoin the yarn to the 1st st from Row 11, ch 1 (not counted as a st), *cdc 2, 2cdc in next st* repeat from * to * 7 times, cdc 3. (31 sts)

Fasten off.

Row 13: With RS facing, rejoin yarn to the 1st st from Row 12, ch 1 (not counted as a st), cdc 31.

Fasten off, weave in all ends.

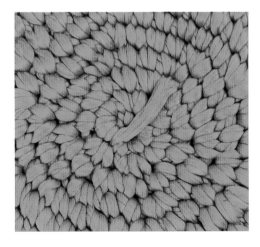

THE HUMBLE PLACEMAT

Simple and timeless, this is a placemat to grace any dining table, whether your style is rustic farmhouse or modern urban. T-shirt yarn is the perfect choice for this project, because of its weight and durability, and with the options of a whole kaleidoscope of shades, you can tailor your yarn choice to complement your colour scheme.

Now, as much as I love a bit of complicated crochetery, I do prefer an unpretentious project and you can't get simpler than this: crochet a circle, add a border.

TOP TIP

T-shirt yarn is one of those more challenging yarns. It can be a dream to work with, but I must warn you, it can also be a tad tricky; you can get thick bits, thin bits, knotty bits, spotty bits, and that can all be in the same bobbin. The yarn can sometimes be stretchy and thick, or fluffy and thin. And unlike spun yarn, there is no standardisation. T-shirt yarn is just T-shirt yarn. But don't let me put you off – it's fab to use, and is perfect for those projects where stability and structure are needed. And if you do come across a strange bit of yarn, simply chop it out and carry on.

OTHER THINGS TO TRY

It goes without saying that your placemat could easily become as large as you please; if you keep increasing the size, you'll end up with a rather wonderful rug!

YOU WILL NEED:

- Crochet hook: 10mm (US N/P/15)
- 1 × bobbin T-shirt yarn (around 300g/10½oz for the placemat, 50g/1¾oz for the coaster)

Yarn alternative:

Any yarn and hook to match

Finished size:

Placemat: 35cm (13¾in)

Coaster: 12cm (4¾in)

You can make your placemat whatever size you choose. Just increase or decrease the circle size (see Crocheting a Flat Circle, in Techniques) before adding the border.

PATTERN

Round 1: ch 4 (ch 3 counts as tr here and throughout), 11tr in 4th ch from hook. Sl st into top of beginning ch-3 to join. (12 sts)

Round 2: ch 3, tr 1 in same st at base of ch-3, 2tr in each st around. Sl st into top of beginning ch-3 to join. (24 sts)

Round 3: ch 3, 2tr in next st,*tr 1, 2tr in next st* repeat from * to * around. Sl st into top of beginning ch-3 to join. (36 sts)

Round 4: ch 3, tr 1, 2tr in next st, *tr 2, 2tr in next st* repeat from * to * around. Sl st into top of beginning ch-3 to join. (48 sts)

Round 5: ch 3, tr 2, 2tr in next st, *tr 3, 2tr in next st* repeat from * to * around. Sl st into top of beginning ch-3 to join. (60 sts)

Round 6: ch 3, tr 3, 2tr in next st, *tr 4, 2tr in next st* repeat from * to * around. Sl st into top of beginning ch-3 to join. (72 sts)

Border: ch 1, beginning in 2nd st from hook, make 1 reverse dc in each st around, sl st into 1st reverse dc to join.

Fasten off, weave in ends.

COASTER

Make Rounds 1–2 from placemat pattern, then add border.

ZIGZAG BLANKET

You can never have too many blankets – that's why there are two of them in the book. This one is cheery and colourful and will brighten up the décor in any room. The zigzags are simply created by regular increases and decreases using treble stitches. It's a soothing pattern which you'll soon have memorised, as there's only one row to repeat backwards and forwards.

TOP TIP

Changing colour is easy. Simply fasten off at the end of the completed row and attach the new colour with a sl st for the first stitch of the next. Tie the ends together (to keep things secure) and then crochet over the ends as you go. That way there'll be nothing to weave in later and you can just snip them carefully away.

OTHER THINGS TO TRY

The world's your oyster with this pattern, there are so many things you could do with it. Why not use up any chunky yarn leftovers and make a fabulous scarf by reducing the number of stitches in the foundation chain and adding lots more rows?

YOU WILL NEED:

- Crochet hook: 15mm (US Q/19)
- 3 × 100g (3½oz) balls each of Schoeller und Stahl Semira in Weiss (shade 01), Rot (shade 03), Graumeliert (shade 12), Pink (shade 17), Fuchsie (shade 18) and Royal (shade 19)
- Tapestry needle

Yarn alternative:

Any yarn and hook to match

Finished size:

116 × 135cm (46 × 53in)

PATTERN

Hold 2 strands together throughout pattern.

Foundation ch: With 15mm hook and Rot, ch 57 (foundation chain must be a multiple of 14 +1).

Row 1: ch 3 (counts as tr here and throughout), tr 1 in 4th ch from hook, tr 5, tr3tog, tr 5, *3tr in next st, tr 5, tr3tog, tr 5* repeat from * to * to last st, 2tr in last st, turn.

Rows 2–29: Repeat Row 1, changing colour in the following order: Pink (Rows 5–9), Fuchsie (Rows 10–14), Weiss (Rows 15–19), Royal (Rows 20–24), Graumeliert (Rows 25–29).

Fasten off and weave in ends.

HEXIE RUG

The best thing about this rug is its versatility. You see, it's made with lots of hexagons, which can be arranged in any shape you choose: long and thin as a floor runner or round-ish like the one pictured. And as for colour – what do you fancy? Make it in one colour, two colours or every colour of the rainbow.

TOP TIP

You might need to change your hook size depending on the elasticity or width of the T-shirt yarn you're working with. This will help get your hexies to the same-ish size. Don't worry too much though, they'll come together nicely once they are joined together.

OTHER THINGS TO TRY

This has to be the perfect pattern for home-made T-shirt yarn, as you only need around 25m (27yd) for each motif. What's more, as the hexies are joined together at the end, you can just keep adding to your rug as you make more yarn.

YOU WILL NEED

- Crochet hook: 15mm (US Q/19) hook; you might need a 12mm (US P/Q-16) too
- 1 × 860g (30oz) approx bobbin each of Hoooked Zpaghetti yarn in White and Red
- 1 × 410g (15oz) approx bobbin each of Tek Tek yarn in Turquoise and Golden
- Tapestry needle

Yarn alternative:

Any T-shirt yarn

Finished size:

Each hexie measures approximately 23cm (9in) in diameter and uses around 25m (27yd) of T-shirt yarn.

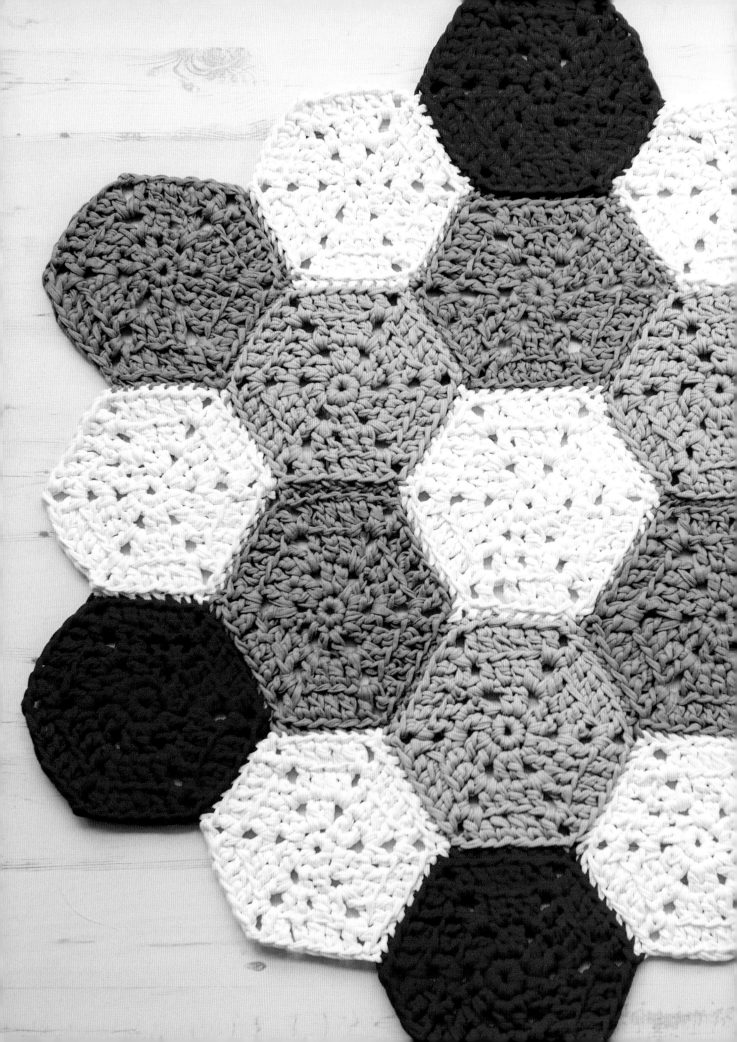

PATTERN

Make as many hexies as you need. I made 19 in total: 7 White, 5 Red, 4 Turquoise and 3 Golden.

Round 1: ch 2, 6dc in 2nd ch from hook. Sl st into 1st dc to join. (6 sts)

Round 2: ch 3 (counts as treble here and throughout), 1tr in same st, ch 1, (2tr, ch 1) in each stitch around. Sl st into top of beginning ch-3 to join. (18 sts).

Round 3: ch 3, tr 1, (tr 1, ch 2, tr 1) in ch-1sp, *tr 2, (tr 1, ch 2, tr 1) in ch-1sp) * repeat from * to * around. Sl st into top of beginning ch-3 to join. (36 sts)

Round 4: ch 3, then in BLO: tr 2, (tr 1, ch 2, tr 1) in ch-2sp, *tr 4, (tr 1, ch 2, tr 1) in ch-2sp* repeat from * to * around, 1 tr in last st. Sl st into top of beginning ch-3 to join. (48 sts)

Note: If you find that your ch 3 at the beginning of each round is a little conspicuous, ch 2 instead – it will still count as a treble, but be less obvious in its finished appearance.

TO JOIN THE HEXIES

Turn the hexies with RS together. Using leftover T-shirt yarn, stitch the back loops together. Repeat until all the sides are joined.

SLOUCHY BEANIE

One of the best things about crocheting with multi-coloured yarn is that it does all the work for you – no colour changes needed – so there's no faffing around with joining in yarn or weaving in ends. Plus, this hat only uses two balls of yarn so it's super-thrifty, too.

TOP TIP

When making hats or scarves, look for yarns with some wool content to keep you cosy. The yarn label will tell you the fibres used and in what percentage – even a little wool goes a long way to warding off the winter chills and needn't cost a fortune.

OTHER THINGS TO TRY

The information that came with the yarn I used recommended a 10mm hook, but I found it didn't create enough drape and the hat certainly wouldn't have been slouchy enough. If you want to substitute the yarn, then look for any which also recommends a 10mm hook.

YOU WILL NEED:

- Crochet hooks: 12mm (US P/Q/16) and 10mm (US N/P/15)
- 2 × 100g (3½oz) balls Stylecraft Swift Knit in Teal (shade 2048)
- Tapestry needle

Yarn alternative:

Any super chunky yarn of a similar weight and meterage

Finished size:

Approximately 30 × 22cm (12 × 8½in)

PATTERN

With 12mm hook, ch 4, join with sl st to make ring.

Round 1: ch 3 (counts as tr here and throughout pattern), 9tr in ring. Sl st into top of beginning ch-3 to join. (10 sts)

Round 2: ch 3, 1fptr around st at base of ch-3, *(1tr, 1fptr) in next st* repeat from * to * around. Sl st into top of beginning ch-3 to join. (20 sts)

Round 3: ch 3, *(1tr, 1fptr) in next st, tr 1* repeat from * to * to last st, (1tr, 1fptr) in last st. Sl st into top of beginning ch-3 to join. (30 sts)

Round 4: ch 3, tr 1, *1fptr in next st, tr 2* repeat from * to * to last st, 1fptr in last st. Sl st into top of beginning ch-3 to join. (30 sts)

Rounds 5–12: Repeat Round 4.

Round 13: change to 10mm hook, repeat Round 4.

Round 14: ch 2 (not counted as a st), htr 30 beginning in same st as beginning ch-2. Sl st into top of 1st htr to join. (30 sts)

Fasten off, weave in ends.

You'll have enough yarn to make a natty pompom, should you want one. If not, then simply leave your hat unadorned.

ENORMOUS FLOOR CUSHION

Take lounging to a new level with this ginormous beanbag. Crocheted in sturdy T-shirt yarn, it's built to stand the tough treatment that family life will (literally) throw at it. It's the perfect recliner to while away the hours with a good book or maybe your favourite crochet project. I'm not going to lie to you, this project is epic. It's big, it's heavy and it's cumbersome. But it fully embodies what supersize crochet is all about and is actually an incredibly easy pattern: a tube of crochet, where one edge is closed horizontally, the other vertically.

TOP TIP

Your arms might ache a bit from working on this project, so work on it slowly and watch it grow over a few days.

OTHER THINGS TO TRY

Alter the size of your floor cushion by adjusting the number of stitches in the foundation chain (any even number of stitches will work) and the number of rows you complete.

YOU WILL NEED:

- Crochet hook: 15mm (US Q/19)
- 2 x 800g (28¼oz) approx bobbins of Jolly Good Yarn in Lime
- 8 x 800g (28¼oz) approx bobbins of Jolly Good Yarn in Grey
- 125-250 litres (4½-9 cubic feet) beanbag pellets depending on the finished size of your bag. Use an online 'beanbag filler calculator' to find a more accurate amount.
- 1m (1yd) of fabric to create a lining (at least 135cm/54in wide)
- Tapestry needle

Yarn alternative:

Any T-shirt yarn and hook to match

Finished size:

85 x 110cm (33½ x 43¼in)

PATTERN

In Lime, ch 96, leaving a 4m (4½yd) tail for stitching closed at the end. Sl st into 1st ch to join (ensuring the chain isn't twisted).

Round 1: ch 1, 1 dc in each st around. (96 sts)

Rounds 2–17*: 1 cdc in each st around.

Round 18: In Grey, 1 cdc in each st around.

Round 19: In Lime, 1 cdc in each st around.

Rounds 20–77*: In Grey, 1 cdc in each st around.

Fasten off.

*or until desired height reached.

TO MAKE UP

Lie your big tube of crochet flat on the floor in front of you, with the RS facing out and the Lime yarn-end to the bottom right. Close the front edge by using the leftover Lime to sl st across, joining the stitches together. Using the cushion measurements as a guide, cut out two pieces of fabric (adding a 1cm/½in seam allowance) and sew together along three sides. Turn seams to inside and fill with beanbag pellets. Sew the final seam closed and insert into cushion. Next, locate the middle stitch of the top and sl st the two sides closed from top to bottom, using the Grey yarn. You should have one horizontal and one vertical seam, creating the wedge shape.

Fasten off and weave in the ends. To make the crochet washable/removable, sl st the top seam together as instructed and fasten off – but do not cut off the ends. Instead, simply push them into the cushion to hide them. When the cushion needs a wash, pull out the ends and undo the stitches until you can remove the inner beanbag. Tie the ends in a loose knot before washing (to prevent the whole seam unravelling).

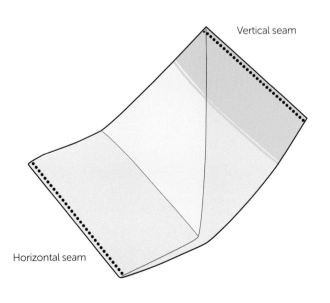

Vertical seam

Horizontal seam

STAR CUSHION

See? Not everything is super-huge and ginormously massive in this book. This sweet little cushion is made using the softest Merino (extreme Merino, obviously) and is a luxury statement cushion for a grand chair. Heck, it would be a luxury statement for a battered old sofa, too!

TOP TIP

This fabulous yarn isn't spun and twisted like other regular yarns and so is very easy to catch whilst you are working with it. To avoid ruining your stitches, you might want to remove your jewellery before you start to crochet.

OTHER THINGS TO TRY

This is another pattern based on a circle, so it's easy to alter the size. Make your circle to the desired circumference (see Crocheting a Flat Circle in Techniques) and then make similar decreases to the ones I have suggested in Rounds 6, 7 and 8. Continue to make decreases until the opening at the back is small enough to sew closed.

YOU WILL NEED:

- Crochet hook: 25mm (US U/50)
- 500g (17½oz) Woolly Mahoosive Petite Merino Super Chunky Yarn in Cream
- 100g (3½oz) stuffing

Yarn alternative:

Any giant yarn and hook to match

Finished size:

28 × 10cm (11 × 4in)

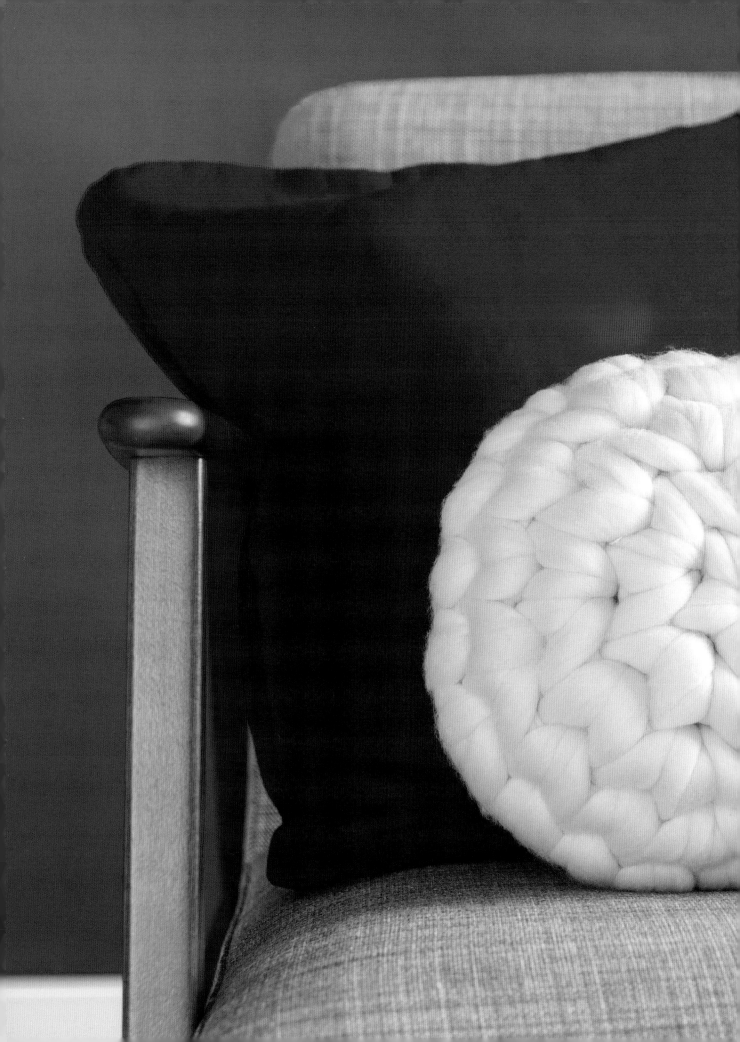

PATTERN

Round 1: 5dc in magic ring or ch 2, 5dc in 2nd ch from hook. (5 sts)

Round 2: 2cdc in each st around. (10 sts)

Round 3: *cdc 1, 2cdc in next st* repeat from * to * around. (15 sts)

Round 4: *cdc 2, 2cdc in next st* repeat from * to * around. (20 sts)

Round 5: *cdc 3, 2cdc in next st* repeat from * to * around. (25 sts)

Round 6: (cdc 1, cdc2tog) 8 times, cdc 1. (17 sts)

Round 7: (cdc2tog) 8 times, cdc 1. (9 sts)

Stuff firmly.

Round 8: (cdc2tog) 3 times (short round – leave remaining sts unworked).

Sew closed (use your fingers) and weave in ends.

COCOON SHRUG

Wrap yourself in the warmest of hugs with this oh-so-simple shrug. Seriously, it may look like the most complicated of pieces, but I'll let you into a little secret... it's just a rectangle of crochet. Yep. A rectangle.

TOP TIP

This is one of those gorgeously light, high-loft yarns, so you'll want to work with a fairly loose tension to avoid squashing all the air out.

OTHER THINGS TO TRY

There's nothing to stop you from making this shrug in whatever yarn, hook and stitch you please. Simply aim for a similar sized rectangle, stitch up the sides to create the sleeves and you're good to go. Or how about adjusting the measurements of your rectangle and changing the size of the shrug? Any length of foundation chain will work, as will any number of rows – a smaller rectangle makes a shoulder shrug, or a bigger rectangle makes a maxi-shrug. It's up to you!

YOU WILL NEED:

- Crochet hook: 20mm (US S/36) for working the shrug, 15mm (US Q/19) for crocheting the seam (optional)
- 6 × 100g (3½oz) balls Rico Fashion Gigantic Mohair in Stone Grey (shade 06)

Yarn alternative:

Any yarn and hook to match – see Other Things to Try

Finished size:

104 × 96cm (41 × 38in) (unfolded)

Adjust the number of stitches and rows to aim for a rectangle of a similar size.

PATTERN

Working from bottom to top, in rows.

Ch 39

Row 1: ch 3 (counts as 1st tr), then beginning in 4th ch from hook, tr 1 in each ch across, turn. (40 sts)

Rows 2–31: ch 1 (not counted as a st), exdc 1 in each st across, turn.

Row 32: ch 3 (counts as 1st tr), tr 1 in each st across.

Fasten off and weave in ends.

TO MAKE UP

With RS facing, fold the top edge over to meet the bottom edge. Use a 15mm (Q/19) hook (or crochet tightly) and sl st the outer edges closed, leaving an 18cm (7in) opening at the end for armholes. If you prefer, you can stitch the sides closed using leftover yarn instead.

CHUNKY SEAT PAD

Make your favourite chair a far more comfortable place to sit by crocheting a gorgeously chunky seat pad. By using mega yarn, this project can be created with a square of stitches and doesn't need any filling to give it its shape.

TOP TIP

To keep the edges of your cushion perfectly neat, this project benefits from the smallest little turning chains you can possibly make at the beginning of each row. To do this, either use a smaller hook, or pull the yarn through using your fingers.

OTHER THINGS TO TRY

Every chair varies in size and yours will probably be different to mine. All you need to do is adjust the number of stitches in your foundation chain and how many rows you complete to make your seat pad a perfect fit.

YOU WILL NEED:

- Crochet hook: 40mm
- 250g (8¾oz) Woolly Mahoosive Wiggly Yarn in Red

Yarn alternative:

Any giant yarn and hook to match

Finished size:

30 × 30cm (12 × 12in)

PATTERN

Ch 8

Row 1: ch 1 (not counted as a st here and throughout), sl st 1 in each st across, turn. (8 sts)

Rows 2–15: ch 1, sl st 1 in each st across, turn.

Fasten off, weave in ends.

COLOUR BLOCK COWL

Think winter. Think snow, ice, freezing winds and minus temperatures. Now imagine yourself cocooned within this mega cowl; warm, cosy and more importantly, on-trend. Worked simply in rows, use up all of your yarn to create as much cowl as you can and then slip stitch the edges together. Simple.

TOP TIP

This yarn is quite high-loft, meaning it can be squished flat when you crochet with it. To avoid this, work with light, loose tension and don't over-tighten your stitches.

OTHER THINGS TO TRY

This is a pattern where you can adjust the size to suit you. Just make sure your foundation chain is an odd number of stitches and the pattern will work perfectly.

YOU WILL NEED:

- Crochet hook: 15mm (US Q/19)
- 2 x 100g (3½oz) balls of Rowan Big Wool in Burnt Orange (shade 51)
- 2 x 100g (3½oz) balls of Rowan Big Wool in Glum (shade 56)
- Tapestry needle

Yarn alternative:

Any yarn and hook to match

Finished size:

Approximately 38 x 70cm (15 x 28in)

PATTERN

Note: The (ch 1, turn) at the beginning of each row is your turning chain and is not counted as a stitch.

Foundation ch: In Burnt Orange, ch 45.

Row 1: (ch 1), dc 1, *ch 1, sk 1 st, dc 1* repeat from * to * across row, turn.

Row 2: (ch 1), dc 1, dc 1 in ch-1sp *ch 1, dc 1 in ch-1sp* repeat from * to * to last st, dc 1 in last stitch, turn.

Row 3: (ch 1), dc 1, ch 1, *dc 1 in ch-1sp, ch 1* repeat from * to * to last st, dc 1 in last stitch, turn.

Rows 4–48 (approx): Repeat Rows 2 and 3 alternately. Change colour to Glum at Row 25, or when you run out of yarn.

Leave enough yarn to join together.

Turn with RS facing and sl st the top and bottom rows together. Fasten off and weave in ends.

TO MAKE UP

Turn with RS facing and sl st the top and bottom rows together. Fasten off and weave in ends.

SCOTTIE DOG CUSHION

Woof, woof! This doggie cushion is the perfect house guest and well-trained too. Crocheted in T-shirt yarn, he'll make the perfect cushion for a bed, a sofa, or an adorable floor cushion. He is crocheted in rows from the tail to the head, and the shaping is achieved by increasing or decreasing stitches at the beginning and ends of the rows.

TOP TIP

If you're like me, then you might live in a house with kids, a husband and a real dog. If that's the case, then things don't stay clean for long and your cushion will need to be washed. To make it washable, double crochet the two pieces closed as instructed and fasten off – but don't cut off the ends. Instead, simply push them inside the cushion to hide them. When the cushion needs to be cleaned, pull out the ends and undo some of the stitching. Tie the end in a loose knot to prevent it all unravelling, then remove the stuffing (this can be washed separately in a pillowcase tied at the top) and wash as per the yarn manufacturer's instructions.

OTHER THINGS TO TRY

This pattern would work in just about any yarn you fancy. Make sure that your hook is a match for the yarn you've chosen and you'll soon be creating canine cushions in all shapes and sizes.

YOU WILL NEED:

- Crochet hook: 15mm (US Q/19)
- 2 × 860g (30oz) approx bobbin of Tek Tek Yarn in Café Latte (I used a small amount of leftover white T-shirt yarn to edge my Scottie, but you will have enough in Café Latte to complete yours)
- 3 × pillows for stuffing (check they meet current safety standards)
- 1.5m (60in) of ribbon
- Tapestry needle

Yarn alternative:

Any yarn and hook to match

Finished size:

Approximately 79cm (31in) wide and 76cm (30in) tall

PATTERN

At the beginning of each row, ch 1 and turn your work.

Foundation ch: ch 27.

Row 1: dc 27.

Row 2: 2dc in first st, dc 25, 2dc in last st. (29 sts)

Row 3: 2dc in first st, dc 28. (30 sts)

Row 4: dc 29, 2dc in last st, ch 1. (32 sts including 1 ch)

Row 5: 2dc in first st, dc 29, dc2tog.

Row 6: 4 sl st, dc 28.

Row 7: (short row) dc 27 (leave 5 sts unworked). (27 sts)

Row 8: dc 27.

Row 9: dc 25, dc2tog. (26 sts)

Rows 10–11: dc 26.

Row 12: (short row) dc 19 (leave 7 sts unworked). (19 sts)

Rows 13–24: dc 19.

Row 25: 2dc in first st, dc 18. (20 sts)

Row 26: 2dc in first st, dc 18, 2dc in last st. (22 sts)

Row 27: 2dc in first st, dc 20, 2dc in last st. (24 sts)

Row 28: 2dc in first st, dc 22, 2dc in last st, ch 3. (29 sts, including 3 ch)

Row 29: dc 28, 2dc in last st, ch 3. (33 sts, including 3 ch)

Row 30: dc 33.

Row 31: dc 31, 2dc in next st, 2dc in last st, ch 5. (40 sts, including 5 ch)

Row 32: dc 40.

Row 33: dc 39, 2dc in last st. (41 sts)

Continue with head.

Row 34: (short row) dc 24 (leave 17 sts unworked). (24 sts)

Row 35: dc 22, dc2tog. (23 sts)

Row 36: 3 sl st, dc 18, dc2tog. (22 sts)

Row 37: (short row) dc2tog, dc 17 (leave 3 sl sts unworked). (18 sts)

Row 38: dc2tog, dc 15, 2dc in last st.

Row 39: 2dc in first st, dc 15, dc2tog.

Row 40: dc2tog, dc 15, 2dc in last st.

Row 41: 2dc in first st, dc 17. (19 sts)

Row 42: dc2tog, dc 17. (18 sts)

Row 43: (short row) 2dc in first st, dc 15 (leave 2 sts unworked). (17 sts)

Rows 44–45: dc 17.

Row 46: (short row) 3 sl st, dc 14.

Row 47: dc 14 (leave 3 sl sts unworked). (14 sts)

Rows 48–49: dc 14.

Fasten off.

FRONT LEG

With WS facing, locate Row 33 of the body and insert hook in 8th stitch from the left and work right to left.

Row 34a: dc 8. (8 sts)

Row 35a: (short row) dc 7 (leave 1 st unworked). (7 sts)

Row 36a: dc2tog, dc 5. (6 sts)

Fasten off.

BACK LEG

With WS facing, locate Row 11 of the body and insert hook in 7th stitch from left and work right to left.

Row 11a: dc 7. (7 sts)

Row 12a: dc 5, dc2tog. (6 sts)

Fasten off.

TO MAKE UP

Choose the better dog-shaped piece to be the front and weave in all ends from both pieces on the inside. Put the two sides together and use a length of T-shirt yarn to double crochet around the edges. Before reaching the end, stuff the cushion firmly, pushing it into all the nooks and crannies, then finish off.

Remember to tie the ribbon in a natty bow around your Scottie's neck, and you're finished.

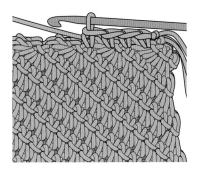

STATEMENT NECKLACE

Knitted and crocheted necklaces have been around for a while. But not like this. This project uses a small amount of T-shirt yarn to create a show-stopping statement piece – perfect for using up any oddments. And what's more, you can make it in about 10 minutes.

TOP TIP

T-shirt yarn does have a bit of stretch, which can take some getting used to. Just remember not to over-tighten your work as you make the stitches and you'll be fine.

OTHER THINGS TO TRY

This would be the perfect project for your own yarn. If you need to adjust the size of the necklace, then simply alter the foundation chain and adjust the number of slip stitches you make either side of the motif pattern in Row 2.

YOU WILL NEED:

- Crochet hook: 12mm (US P/Q/16)
- 15m (16yd) of Hoooked Zpaghetti Yarn in Violet

Yarn alternative:

Any T-shirt yarn

Finished size:

Approximately 55 × 6cm (22 × 2⅜in)

PATTERN

Leave a 30cm (12in) tail at beginning.

Foundation ch: ch 33

Row 1: dc 32 beginning in 2nd ch from hook. Ch 2, turn 180 degrees to work Row 2 along the other side of the chain.

Row 2: sl st 8, dc 2, 2htr in next st, tr 2, 2tr in next st, dtr 4, 2tr in next st, tr 2, 2htr in next st, dc 2, sl st 8. (36 sts)

Fasten off, leaving a 30cm (12in) tail at end. Use tails from each end of the necklace to tie around your neck.

OMBRE CIRCLES TOTE BAG

Carry everything you need in this perfectly-sized bag. It's based on a giant circular-centred granny square motif and crocheted by holding two strands of yarn together, making this project super-easy and super-speedy. Working with chunky yarn also means that you don't have to stitch in a fabric lining, although you can find some great tutorials online if you'd like to.

TOP TIP

Handle length is easily adjusted by increasing or decreasing the number of chain stitches in Round 2 of the handles pattern. You can also make a wider base by adding another row or two to the sides/base pattern.

OTHER THINGS TO TRY

Why not make a huge blanket? Simply make lots of the square motifs and stitch them together. Or how about a cushion? All you'll need is two of the squares, joined along the sides. It couldn't be easier.

YOU WILL NEED:

- Crochet hook: 15mm (US Q/19)
- 2 × 200g (7oz) balls Stylecraft Special XL in Graphite (shade 3060)
- 1 × 200g (7oz) ball Stylecraft Special XL in Duck Egg (shade 1820), Cream (shade 3055), Sage (shade 3056), and Petrol (shade 3059)
- Tapestry needle

Yarn alternative:

Any super chunky yarn and hook to match

Finished size:

34 × 34cm (13½ × 13½in) (excluding handle)

PATTERN

Hold 2 strands together throughout pattern.

FRONT/BACK (MAKE 2)

Round 1: In Cream, ch 4 (counts as tr and ch 1), 9tr in 4th ch from hook. Sl st into top of beginning ch-3 to join. (10 sts)

Round 2: In Duck Egg, ch 3 (counts as tr here and throughout), tr 1 in same st at base of ch-3, 2tr in each st around. Sl st into top of beginning ch-3 to join. (20 sts)

Round 3: In Sage, ch 3, 2tr in next st, *tr 1, 2tr in next st* repeat from * to * around. Sl st into top of beginning ch-3 to join. (30 sts)

Round 4: In Petrol, ch 3, tr 1, 2tr in next st, *tr 2, 2tr in next st* repeat from * to * around. Sl st into top of beginning ch-3 to join. (40 sts)

Round 5: In Graphite working all sts in BLO, ch 3, (tr 1, ch 2, 2tr) in same st at base of ch-3, tr 1, htr 2, dc 3, htr 2, tr 1, *(2tr, ch 2, 2tr) in next st, tr 1, htr 2, dc 3, htr 2, tr 1* repeat from * to * 3 times. Sl st into top of beginning ch-3 to join. (60 sts).

Fasten off.

SIDES/BASE (MAKE 1)

Foundation ch: In Graphite, ch 45.

Rows 1–2: ch 1 (not counted as a st), dc 1 in each st, turn.

Fasten off.

TO MAKE UP

Join the side to the front/back panels by holding the pieces with WS facing. Simply double crochet the two pieces together, through the FLO of the front/back stitches and both loops of the side panel stitches. Don't cut your yarn – you will carry on with the pattern.

TOP EDGE AND HANDLE

Turn the bag right side out, with the side edge facing you. Work along the stitches at the top in a clockwise direction.

Round 1: ch 1, then beginning in the same st *dc 2 along side, dc 1 in ch-2sp, dc 13 (BLO) along front/back edge, dc 1 in ch-2sp* repeat from * to *. Sl st into 1st dc to join. (34 sts)

Round 2: ch 1, then beginning in same st, dc 4, ch 20, sk next 11 sts, dc 6, ch 20, sk next 11 sts, dc 2. Sl st into 1st dc to join.

Round 3: sl st 3, 28 dc in ch-20sp, sl st 6, 28 dc in ch-20sp, sl st 2. Sl st into 1st sl st to join.

Fasten off, weave in ends.

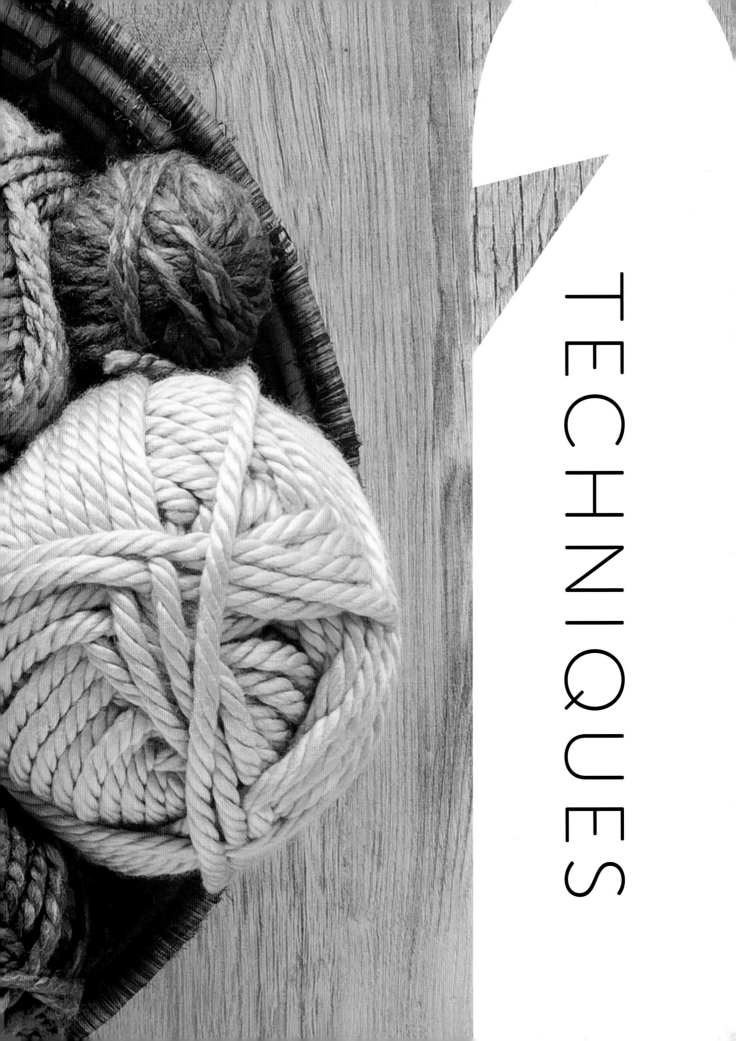

TECHNIQUES

ABBREVIATIONS

*: indicates a repeat sequence (repeat stitches in between asterisks as many times as stated)

BLO: back loops only

cdc: centre double crochet

cdc2tog: centre double crochet 2 stitches together (to decrease 1 stitch)

ch: chain

ch-sp: chain space (a number indicates how many chain stitches there are)

dc: double crochet

dc2tog: double crochet 2 stitches together (to decrease 1 stitch)

dtr: double treble crochet

exdc: extended double crochet

FLO: front loop only

fptr: front post treble crochet

htr: half treble crochet

RS: right side

sk: skip

sl st: slip stitch

st/s: stitch/es

tr: treble crochet

tr2tog: treble crochet 2 stitches together

tr3tog: treble crochet 3 stitches together

WS: wrong side

CROCHET TERMS

Be aware that crochet terms in the US are different from those in the UK. This can be confusing as the same terms are used to refer to different stitches under each system.

The list here gives a translation of UK terms to US terms:

UK	US
slip stitch	slip stitch
double crochet	single crochet
half treble crochet	half double crochet
treble crochet	double crochet
double treble crochet	treble crochet
triple treble crochet	double treble crochet

GETTING STARTED

THE STARTING LOOP OR SLIPKNOT

Before you begin, you will need to make your first stitch. This will form the basis for all the following stitches. Make a loop near the cut end of the yarn and insert the crochet hook into the loop, picking up the end of the yarn leading to the ball. Draw this new loop of yarn through the existing loop, and gently pull on the end of the yarn leading to the ball to tighten this new loop around the hook. This is the slipknot and does not count as a stitch.

MAGIC RING

The magic ring is an alternative way to begin crocheting in the round. In contrast to working into a chain or a chain circle, the basic magic ring allows you to tighten the first row, eliminating any opening.

To make a magic ring, make a loop about 10cm (a few inches) from the end of your yarn. Grasp the join of the loop (where the two strands of yarn overlap) between your left thumb and forefinger. Insert hook into the loop from front to back. Draw up a loop.

Ch 1 (does not count as st).

Insert hook into the loop, so you are crocheting over the loop and the yarn tail. Draw up a loop to begin your first dc of Round 1. Complete the dc. Continue to crochet over the loop and the yarn tail until you have the required number of dc for your first round. Grab the yarn tail and pull to draw the centre of the ring tightly closed. Begin your second round by crocheting into the first stitch of the first round.

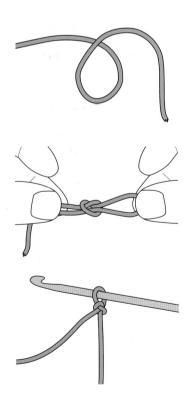

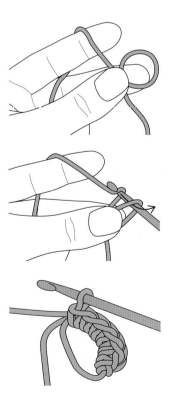

INVISIBLE FASTENING OFF

This is a really handy trick to have up your crocheter's sleeve as it gives a perfect finish to projects, especially when you're working in rounds.

1. When you have completed the last stitch of the piece, cut the yarn, leaving a tail of around 20cm (8in) and pull this through the stitch.

2. Thread the yarn onto your needle and insert your needle through the top of the next stitch (in the same way that you would insert your hook) and then back into the top of the stitch you have just come from. This makes a faux stitch, creating the invisible finish.

3. Weave the tail into the back of your work and snip the end away.

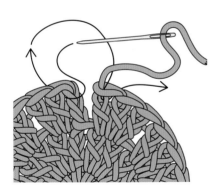

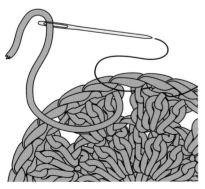

CROCHETING A FLAT CIRCLE

Crocheting a circle is one of those techniques which is a must for all crocheters and the basis of many a pattern. This book is no different and you'll find plenty of examples of projects beginning in the round. If you know how to alter the size of a circle, then you'll be able to personalise the projects to suit you; perhaps turning the bag pattern into a rug? Or a coaster into a cushion? I can promise you there's no secret to this. There is a formula and it's easy:

1. Make xx number of stitches into a magic ring or ch 2 and make xx number of stitches into the second ch from your hook.

2. Make 2 sts in each stitch around.

3. *Make 1 st in the next st, then 2 sts in the next st* repeat from * to * around.

4. *Make 1 st in each of the next 2 sts, then 2 sts in the next st* repeat from * to * around.

5. *Make 1 st in each of the next 3 sts, then 2 sts in the next st* repeat from * to * around.

6. *Make 1 st in each of the next 4 sts, then 2 sts in the next st* repeat from * to * around.

I bet you can see what's going on here and how the pattern will continue. So if I start my circle with 5 stitches in the first round, I will have 10 sts in the second, 15 in the third, 20 in the fourth and so on... (knowing my times tables has never been so useful).

It's all well and good knowing the theory, but sometimes things don't work in practice, especially when you're dealing with stretchy, or textured yarn, or tall stitches. Use this formula as a guide. If your circle starts to curl upwards (not enough stitches) then add a few more increases. If it starts to ripple (too many stitches) then leave out the increases.

CROCHET STITCHES

CHAIN
(abbreviation = ch)

1. Take the yarn over the hook, wrapping it from the back, up over the hook towards the front, and then down and under the hook (every time the yarn is taken over the hook it should be done in this way).

2. Now draw this new loop of yarn through the loop on the hook to complete the chain stitch.

SLIP STITCH
(abbreviation = sl st)

1. Insert the hook into the work at the required point.

2. Take the yarn over the hook and draw this new loop through both the work and the loop on the hook to complete the slip stitch.

DOUBLE CROCHET
(abbreviation = dc)

1. Start by inserting the hook into the work at the required point.

2. Take the yarn over the hook and draw this new loop of yarn through the loop onto the hook – there are now two loops on the hook. Take the yarn over the hook again and draw this new loop through both the loops on the hook. This completes the double crochet stitch.

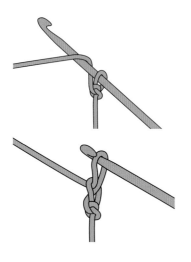

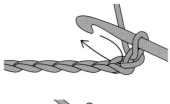

DOUBLE CROCHET DECREASE
(abbreviation = dc2tog)

1. Insert hook into next stitch, wrap the yarn around the hook and draw it back through the stitch (two loops on hook).

2. Insert hook into next stitch.

3. Wrap the yarn around the hook and draw it back through the stitch (three loops on hook). Wrap the yarn around the hook and draw it through all three loops to complete the double crochet decrease.

TREBLE CROCHET
(abbreviation = tr)

1. Wrap the yarn around the hook before inserting it into the work. Wrap the yarn around the hook again and draw this loop through the work – there are now three loops on the hook.

2. Wrap the yarn around the hook once more and draw this new loop through just the first two loops on the hook – the original loop and this new loop.

3. Wrap the yarn around the hook again and draw this new loop through both loops on the hook to complete the treble stitch.

HALF TREBLE
(abbreviation = htr)

1. Start in exactly the way a treble is made until there are three loops on the hook.

2. Wrap the yarn around the hook once more and draw this new loop through all three loops on the hook to complete the half treble stitch.

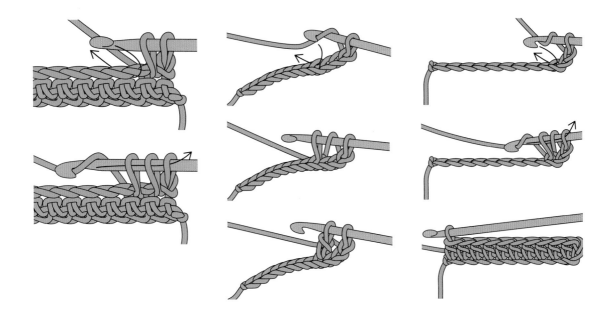

DOUBLE TREBLE
(abbreviation = dtr)

1. Yarn over twice and insert your hook into the stitch. Yarn over and pull the yarn through the stitch.

2. Yarn over and pull the yarn through the first two loops on your hook three times.

FRONT POST TREBLE
(abbreviation = fptr)

1. Yarn over and insert your hook from front to back and front again around the post of the stitch from the row below. Yarn over and pull the yarn back around the post of the stitch (three loops on hook).

2. Yarn over and pull the yarn through the first two loops, (two loops on hook), yarn over and pull the yarn through the last two loops.

CENTRE DOUBLE CROCHET
(abbreviation = cdc)

Sometimes called Waistcoat or Split Stitch, this is just like making a normal double crochet, except you insert your hook into the vertical 'V' of the post of the stitch itself, instead of under the horizontal top loops.

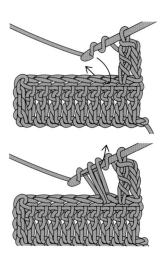

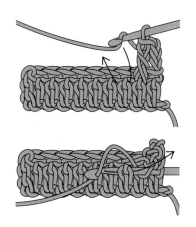

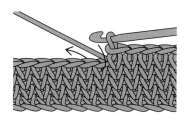

CENTRE DOUBLE CROCHET 2 TOGETHER

(abbreviation = cdc2tog)

1. Insert your hook into the vertical 'V' of the post of the first stitch. Yarn over hook, pull yarn through stitch (two loops on hook).

2. Insert your hook into the vertical 'V' of the post of the next stitch. Yarn over hook, pull yarn through stitch (three loops on hook).

3. Yarn over hook, pull the yarn through all three loops.

EXTENDED DOUBLE CROCHET

(abbreviation = exdc)

1. Insert hook into stitch. Yarn over hook, pull yarn through stitch (two loops on hook).

2. Yarn over hook, pull yarn through one loop (two loops on hook).

3. Yarn over hook, pull yarn through both loops.

REVERSE DOUBLE CROCHET (CRAB STITCH)

1. Insert hook into next stitch to the right, from front to back, with the hook facing downwards.

2. Yarn over hook, pull yarn back through the stitch (two loops on hook).

3. Yarn over hook, pull through both loops on the hook.

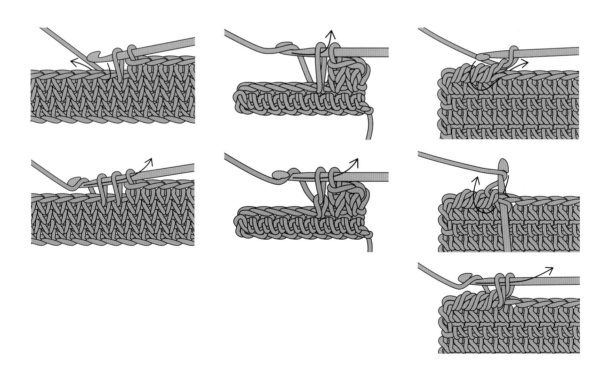

TREBLE 2 TOGETHER
(abbreviation = tr2tog)

1. Yarn over hook, hook into first stitch, yarn over hook, pull yarn through the stitch, yarn over hook, pull the yarn through the first two loops (two loops on hook).

2. Yarn over hook, hook into next stitch, yarn over hook, pull yarn through the stitch, yarn over hook, pull the yarn through the first two loops (three loops on hook).

3. Yarn over hook, pull the yarn through all three loops.

TREBLE 3 TOGETHER
(abbreviation = tr3tog)

1. Repeat Steps 1 and 2 from tr2tog.

2. Yarn over hook, hook into next stitch, yarn over hook, pull yarn through the stitch, yarn over hook, pull the yarn through the first two loops (four loops on hook).

3. Yarn over hook, pull the yarn through all four loops.

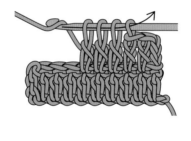

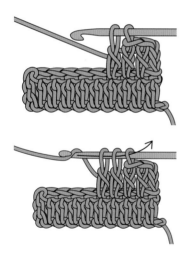

SUPPLIERS

Woolly Mahoosive

www.woollymahoosive.com

Doodlestop

www.doodlestop.co.uk

T-shirt Yarn Shop

www.tshirtyarnshop.co.uk

Love Crochet

www.lovecrochet.com

Stylecraft Yarns

www.stylecraft-yarns.co.uk

DMC Creative World

www.dmccreative.co.uk

Sew and So

www.sewandso.co.uk

ABOUT THE AUTHOR

Sarah is a crocheter, designer, author and blogger who lives with her family in a small village in West Sussex. She taught herself to crochet a few years back and began writing a blog to record her progress.

These days she designs for craft and crochet magazines, and sells crochet patterns in her Etsy shop, www.etsy.com/uk/shop/AnnaboosHouse, as well as offering lots of free patterns and tutorials on her blog, annabooshouse.blogspot.com.

Her first book, *Beginner's Guide to Crochet*, was published in 2015, and *Extreme Crochet* followed in the same year.

Sarah loves to use social media so why not find out what she's working on and say hello at **www.instagram.com/annaboos_house**.

ACKNOWLEDGMENTS

Thanks to all the gals and guys at F&W for making *Supersize Crochet* as awesome as I hoped it would be. To Sarah for enabling this book to happen and Anna for bringing everything together so beautifully. To Jason for his amazing photography, and Kang for his perfect and clear illustrations. Thanks also to Jane and Lynne, for making sure everything I've written makes sense. Thanks a million to my family, especially my husband, Kevin, and my children, Thomas and Annabelle, who allow me the time and space to work and who never complain about the yarn all over the house.

INDEX

A SEWANDSO BOOK
© F&W Media International, Ltd 2017

SewandSo is an imprint of F&W Media International, Ltd
Pynes Hill Court, Pynes Hill, Exeter, EX2 5AZ

F&W Media International, Ltd is a subsidiary of F+W Media, Inc
10151 Carver Road, Suite #200, Blue Ash, OH 242, USA

Text and Designs © Sarah Shrimpton 2017
Layout and Photography © F&W Media International, Ltd 2017

First published in the UK and USA in 2017

Sarah Shrimpton has asserted her right to be identified as author of this work in accordance with the Copyright, Designs and Patents Act, 1988.

A catalogue record for this book is available from the British Library.

ISBN-13: 978-1-4463-0659-8 paperback
SRN: R4954 paperback

ISBN-13: 978-1-4463-7525-9 PDF
SRN: R6118 PDF

ISBN-13: 978-1-4463-7524-2 EPUB
SRN: R6119 EPUB

Printed in China by RR Donnelley for:
F&W Media International, Ltd
Pynes Hill Court, Pynes Hill, Exeter, EX2 5AZ

10 9 8 7 6 5 4 3 2 1

Content Manager: Sarah Callard
Senior Editor: Jeni Hennah
Project Editor: Jane Trollope
Proofreader: Cheryl Brown
Design Manager: Anna Wade
Junior Designer: Ali Stark
Photographer: Jason Jenkins
Production Manager: Beverley Richardson

F&W Media publishes high quality books on a wide range of subjects.
For more great book ideas visit: www.sewandso.co.uk

Layout of the digital edition of this book may vary depending on reader hardware and display settings.

CLAIM YOUR FREE CRAFT EBOOK!

Download a fabulous **FREE EBOOK** from our handpicked selection at:
http://ideas.sewandso.co.uk/free-ebooks

Where crafters come to shop...

Find everything you need for your next craft project amongst thousands of products in needlecraft, sewing, knitting and more.

INTERNATIONAL SHIPPING

NEXT-DAY DELIVERY

DEDICATED CUSTOMER SERVICES TEAM

EARN LOYALTY POINTS AS YOU SHOP

www.**sewandso**.co.uk

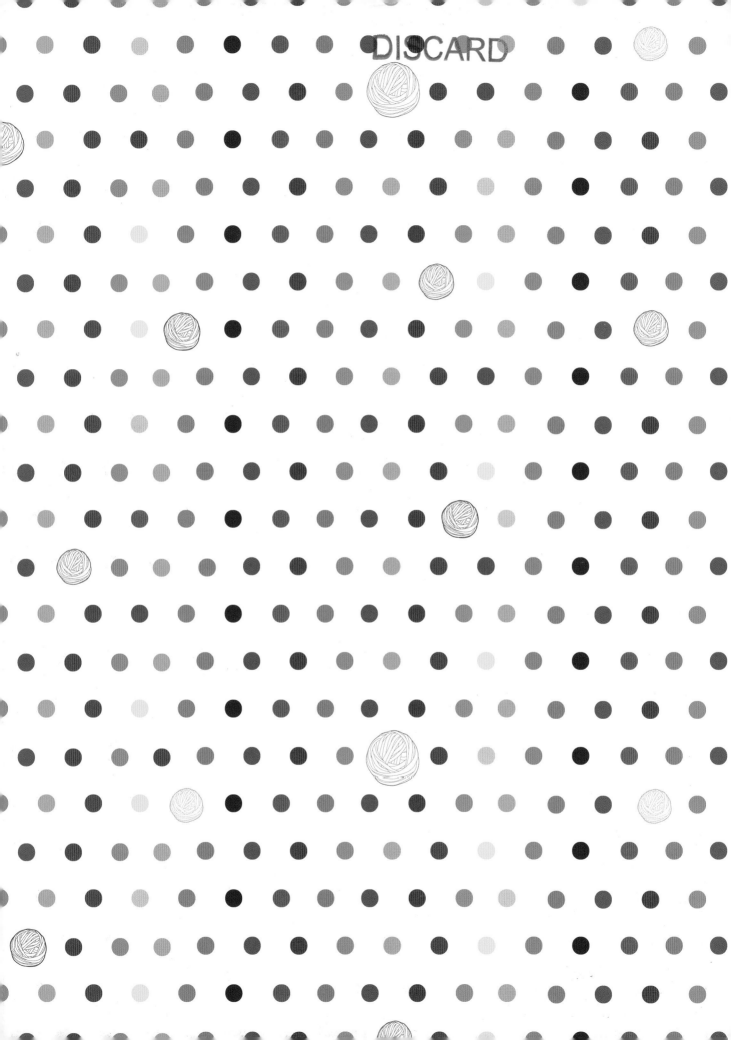